The Marriage Triangle

Leona Sumrall Murphy

PUBLICATION

Unless otherwise indicated,
all Scripture quotations are taken from
the *King James Version* of the Bible.

Marriage Is A Triangle
ISBN O-937580-40-6
Copyright © 1984 by Lester Sumrall
Evangelistic Association
Published by LeSEA Publishing Company
P.O. Box 12
South Bend, Indiana 46624

Printed in the United States of America.
All rights reserved under international
Copyright Law. Contents and/or cover may
not be reproduced in whole or in part in any
form without the express written consent of
the Publisher.

CONTENTS

1. Marriage Is A Triangle..........10
2. Meet My Jim..................13
3. Jim Proposes.................21
4. Pastoring In Rochester.........26
5. The Crossroad................33
6. Our Wedding Day.............41
7. The Unequal Yoke............46
8. In-Laws.....................51
9. Building A Christian Home......57

Introduction

God ordained marriage and everything He created is beautiful. A happy marriage does not come accidentally and neither does it happen overnight. Both partners must make a quality decision to put God's Word in first place. When we stand on the principles the Lord has laid down in his Word, we are sure to have good results. When we know what His Word says about marriage, we can act and speak carefully.

Marriage is a beautiful union in God's eyes. But in the courts of our land marriage is simply a legal contract which can be legally broken, leaving either party to freely marry again.

Marriage is a spiritual contract, a miraculous union. In the marriage union, a bride and a groom are joined together not only in body and soul but spiritually as well. A husband and wife form the strongest bond there is between two human beings. The marriage is much more than a man and a woman just saying, "I do." It is a serious relationship in God's eyes and is not to be entered into lightly.

The consistent Christian behavior in the home is the key to a successful marriage. The man and woman must make a decision that this home is going to be a place of refuge, a place of peace, a place of harmony and beauty.

Next to my relationship with God, making my marriage a success was most important. Married life requires continued understanding. If couples would bring the same planning, the same wisdom, the same assessment into their marriage as they do to their business, many of our domestic problems would be solved. But most men and women put very little effort into their marriages.

1

MARRIAGE IS A TRIANGLE

"And the LORD God said, It is not good that the man should be alone; I will make him an help meet for him."

Genesis 2:18

Marriage is like a triangle—you, your spouse, and God. God ordained marriage and he intends for our marriages to be successful.

God created one man for one woman. This is the happiest mode of living. To break God's moral order is to destroy your own happiness.

The marriage contract is found in Genesis 2:23-24, "And Adam said, This is now bone of my bones, and flesh of my flesh: she shall be called Woman, because she was taken out of Man. Therefore shall a man leave his father and his mother, and shall cleave unto his wife: and they shall be one flesh."

The closest human relationship is marriage. It is more binding than that of parent and child because the two become one flesh.

There must be a relationship between you, your companion, and God. We must have a spiritual relationship with Jesus Christ if the marriage is to be a success.

As the marriage vows are pronounced in faith, the power of God goes into operation. The two believers release their faith: God honors their faith and unites them by His power. The result is a threefold union—the man and woman are not only joined together physically, but also spiritually by God, which makes a perfect triangle.

We read in Genesis 1:1, "In the beginning God created the heaven and the earth." Shall we draw a straight line and call it G O D.

Then we will make another line and call it M A N. In Genesis 2:18, "And the LORD

God said, It is not good that the man should be alone; I will make him an help meet for him." Verses 21-23 read, "And the LORD God caused a deep sleep to fall upon Adam, and he slept: and he took one of his ribs, and closed up the flesh instead thereof; And the rib, which the LORD God had taken from man, made he a woman, and brought her unto the man. And Adam said, This is now bone of my bones, and flesh of my flesh: she shall be called Woman, because she was taken out of Man."

We add a third line, <u>WOMAN</u>. It takes the three to make a perfect triangle.

My brother, Lester Sumrall, gives another triangle which we must have to have a perfect marriage. When he performs a wedding, he explains to the bride and groom that they are to be united in three areas—spirit, soul, and body.

First, there is the body marriage, which is the physical union. We have witnessed multitudes of marriages which are consummated because of sexual desires, physical attraction, a sweet smile or a tender touch. But physical attraction will not hold two people together. In a matter of months they will more than likely find themselves in a divorce court, hating their mate.

To be physically married means that only one-third of the marriage vow is consummated.

Then we have a soul marriage when the mind, emotions, and will are in agreement. Many marriages include not only physical attraction, but also soulish togetherness. The man and woman give consideration to their thinking alike, their emotional compatibility and their willingness to be subservient one to the other by their willpower. This is an important goal in marriage and contributes to their happiness.

To have a spirit marriage is to be one in conversion, faith, and worship. We must be sure that physical attraction is present and that the soulish elements are compatible, but it is most important that we have unity of Christian commitment. The couple must enjoy the same kind of worship and establish a family altar with Bible reading and prayer.

Truly happy marriages are those where MIND, EMOTIONS, and WILL harmonize together and where the bride and groom have spiritual compatibility.

2

MEET MY JIM

The telephone rang . . .

"A long distance call for Leona Sumrall."

"This is she."

"Go ahead, sir..."

"Hello, this is Jim."

"Hi Jim. How are you?"

"Not too happy, I didn't get a letter today!" During the course of our conversation Jim repeated a statement he had made several times before. "Honey, believe me when I say there is something supernatural involved in our being brought together."

My mind was racing furiously. Jim was making himself vulnerable for a deep hurt. Why would he deliberately put himself in such a position? I told him he was going too fast for me. Though Jim appeared to be by nature an easygoing relaxed person, I soon learned he could also be determined. I kept stalling. Finally, Jim said, "I feel the Lord has brought us together. He has given me a love for you that overwhelms me, and I am ready and eager to marry you as soon as possible."

I said, "Jim, you may have your word from God, but He hasn't spoken to me yet. I appreciate you as a Christian, but I'm not yet ready to make a decision about marriage."

My emotions were in turmoil. I was facing the ultimate question. Was I going to give the rest of my life solely to the ministry or did it also include Jim and marriage? The question being, was I ready for such a commitment? I began to pray almost desperately for help and guidance.

Meet My Jim

When I first met Jim he was a serviceman from Tulsa, Oklahoma, stationed at the Air Force base in Alexandria, Louisiana. I had accepted an invitation to conduct a revival meeting in the church he attended. He lived in the same housing complex the church used to lodge its visiting speakers, so it was natural that we should meet.

How well I remember the first time I saw Jim. He was standing on the church steps talking to two men. The pastor said, "Those men have been fasting for this revival."

I tried to cancel the meeting in Alexandria, Louisiana, three different times. I was in the northern part of the state having a tremendous moving of God in our services. The meeting had reached a peak. All I had to do was read the Bible, make a few comments, give an invitation and people would fill the altar. The meeting had gone on for seven weeks. The pastor insisted we stay the eighth week. I told him I wouldn't disappoint the pastor in Alexandria, as I had changed the date for the meeting three times. If I should cancel this date, the pastor would have to release me altogether. The pastor asked permis-

permission to phone the minister in Alexandria, saying, "If he agrees to cancel the meeting, will you stay another week?"

He contacted the pastor but with no success. The minister in Alexandria said, "NO, not on your life. This evangelist promised me a meeting over a year ago. We have been willing to cancel several times so your church could be blessed. God has given you a successful meeting and now it is our turn. We have the advertisement ready."

The following Saturday we drove to Alexandria. The pastor's wife had prepared a nice meal. After visiting for awhile, they took us to the apartment located two blocks from the church. The pastor told us that Brother Jim Murphy, one of the young men from the church, lived in one of the units. "He is an Air Force man," said the pastor. "Feel free to call on him whenever you need anything. He is a good Christian."

I didn't feel that I needed any help. I had cared for myself and Mother Sumrall for many years. All I was interested in was preaching a successful revival. I wanted to see souls saved.

Meet My Jim

On Sunday morning the pastor announced that those who had time should cook a roast or bake a cake or pie, and take it to the evangelist.

A few days later the door bell rang. It was one of the church members bringing a container. She placed it on the table, saying, "I brought a baked ham." It was covered with pineapple rings, cloves, and cooked to a beautiful golden brown. We invited her to sit down and during the conversation she asked, "Have you met Brother Jim Murphy? He lives in one of the apartments." I said, "Yes, the pastor introduced him to Mother and me." She said, "My daughter is in love with him. She has been praying for a dedicated Christian husband. She is now 18 and wants to get married. She has made herself available to him, but for some reason he hasn't responded." She wondered what to do to attract him and let him know she wanted to date him. She said, "You might tell him that my daughter is in love with him. He is the kind of man she had always wanted to marry."

That evening Jim came in from the air base. Mother said, "I feel I should invite the young man in to have a glass of tea and a ham sandwich." I said, "I would leave him alone. I don't think he would want to come back here." "Oh, yes," she said, "a young man that is away from home would enjoy home-cooked food." She went down the hall and invited him to our apartment for a ham sandwich and glass of iced tea. With a big smile, he said, "I would enjoy that." He sat at the end of the table and Mother sat next to him. I was studying at the opposite end preparing my sermon for that evening.

I was provoked with my mother for inviting him. I felt I needed the last hour before church to be alone to get my thoughts together for the service. We had only one table so I had to sit and listen to their conversation.

They talked about miracles and the things that God desired for His people. They were laughing and praising the Lord. Mother burst into tongues and Jim joined her. They were having a good time. I thought to myself, "He is a nice young fellow." But I hoped Mother wouldn't invite him back.

Then I thought about the girl who was in love with him. I decided that I was going to talk to him the following day. If he asked how I knew about the girl, I would tell him the truth - that the girl's mother asked me to mention it to him.

The following afternoon when it was time for him to come from the air base, I sat on the porch swing, waiting for him. As he entered, he stopped to speak. He had a magazine in his hand and asked if he could sit down and show me pictures of the different airplanes they had on that base. I knew nothing about airplanes and I didn't know any more when he finished than I did before he started.

He said, "We prayed several weeks before you came for this revival." I asked, "Have you noticed the young lady that attends each night with dark hair and big brown eyes? I think she is a beautiful girl." He said, "Yes, she is." I smiled and said, "I heard that she is deeply in love with you." Jim looked at me with surprise and almost scorn. He said, "She is NOT my type. That young lady has one thing on her mind and that is getting married." With a stern look on his face, he continued, "I am not interested." It was a rebuke! Who was I to play cupid? I apologized and told him I didn't realize the situation.

With a very serious look on his face, he said, "I want to be a minister. It takes a special kind of girl to be a minister's wife. An overwhelming number of marriages end up in divorce. I do not feel that is the way God intended marriage to be." With that statement, he went into his apartment.

3

JIM PROPOSES

Since I had been invited by a Full-Gospel organization in Cuba to speak at their annual convention, I closed the meeting in Alexandria after three weeks in order to make preparations for my trip. (This was before Fidel Castro came to power, so the island nation was still open to the Christian Gospel.)

Jim became interested in my missionary trip. At the Air Force Base he went to his buddies that had been saved and asked if they would make a donation to help pay for my expenses to Cuba. Most of the men were happy to give. Jim brought the money to the apartment the night before we left.

He asked about our next meeting. I said, "We plan to be in Shreveport tomorrow night for a missionary rally." He replied, "I have two days off. I can drive your car and that way you can conserve your strength for the meeting." My Mother thought it was a great idea.

As we drove along, I studied this young man sitting beside me. He was six feet tall, dark hair, and had an athletic figure. His gray-blue eyes were direct and warm. He was a good conversationalist, probing my life style as a lady preacher. There were times he chuckled rather self-consciously, but I could see he was a caring man, affectionate, and comfortable to be with. He talked about his dreams of being a minister some day.

One week before leaving for Cuba, I received a letter from Jim. In it he wrote,

> "The first time I saw you, God told me you were the one He had chosen for me."

He expressed his great admiration for Mother Sumrall and me. He went on to say,

> "I joined the Air National Guard not knowing the Korean War would

break out. The government federalized my unit. On my way to Alexandria, Louisiana, the bus stopped in Shreveport for two hours. Some of the men walked up town, but I walked out on the bridge crossing the Red River. I had bought a new car. I felt it was time for me to settle down and get married. I began to cry and pray. I was downhearted and depressed. Standing on the bridge looking over the rail, I watched a river boat float downstream. My tears fell in the river as I told the Lord I did not want to be in this war. Not that I didn't love my country but I had served in the army one year previous to this. I was still looking at the river when God spoke to me. 'The girl you want to marry is not my choice for your life. She will not do one thing to promote your ministry. I have a girl for you.' When I saw you, God told me you were the one he had picked out for me. I know you are the one! I am in love with you. Will you marry me?"

I read the letter to my uncle. I laughed and said, "I am not ready to get married." My uncle replied, "Be careful, he is a good man and a good Christian. You can thank God that he admires you and wants to marry you." I said, "That may be true, but I am not interested in marriage. I want to work for the Lord." Jimmy knew the date I would be leaving Mobile, Alabama, for the meeting in Cuba. He was there to say good-bye. I didn't quite understand why he had made this long drive to see me off. He asked me if I would write to him. I said, "I will be busy, but I will try." I told him I appreciated the offering he raised among his friends. While in Cuba I did write two letters telling him about the meeting and the beautiful response of the people. When I came back to the States, I picked up my car in Mobile, Alabama, and Mother and I returned to Springfield, Missouri.

One afternoon I was standing by the window looking down the street. Jim was walking up the sidewalk. I told Mother, "You will not believe who I see walking this way." She looked and said, "That's Jim Murphy and he is coming here!" He walked up on the porch and rang the door bell.

Mother was happy to see him and made

Jim Proposes

him feel welcome. They sat down on the couch and he and Mother had a wonderful time as usual, while I sat across the room in a chair thumbing through a magazine. It seemed hard to believe that two people could talk continually for hours and yet they seemed to have scarcely started on the subjects that interested the two of them.

They talked about my trip to Cuba and the many souls that were saved and filled with the Holy Spirit and those that were healed. You would think Mother made the trip to Cuba. Most of the day he and mother visited together and I cooked the evening meal. Later in the evening, Jim asked if the two of us could walk to a nearby park. We found a bench near the pool and watched the people as they splashed in the water. Soon he began to express his love for me. "I can't get you off my mind. I am unable to sleep or eat because of my love for you. I am sincere when I say I love you with all my heart and have a desire for us to be married." I explained there were "many reasons" why we should NOT consider marriage. The following day Jim had to return to the air base.

4

PASTORING IN ROCHESTER

A few days later, Mother and I went to visit my brother, Lester Sumrall, and his family, who pastored a church in South Bend, Indiana. On Saturday, my brother received a telephone call from Rochester, Indiana. Their pastor had resigned and they needed a minister to fill the pulpit on Sunday. He told the deacon that he did not know of a minister he could contact at that late date. "However, my sister Leona is visiting our home. It is possible I could ask her to come." The deacon had heard me preach in the South Bend church and was pleased that I was available.

In the Sunday morning service the Holy

Spirit moved in a beautiful way. That afternoon the deacons came to the home where we were staying and asked if I would preach a week of revival. I told them I would. The meeting was successful and at the end of the week the deacons asked if I would consider being their pastor. After I had prayed, I agreed to accept the church if I could keep my appointment in Shreveport, Louisiana. For several years we had an annual New Year's Revival for Glad Tidings Assembly beginning on New Year's Eve night and continuing for three weeks. The church agreed that I should keep my commitment. I was able to secure a pastor in my absence.

Lester had resigned the South Bend church to go to the Philippines. He made plans to leave the last of May or the first of June. This gave him four months to itinerate before going oversees. We were invited to spend Christmas with him and his family.

In Lester's home holidays are really celebrated. They make Christmas a big event. His wife always had a well decorated tree with tinsel and lights and loaded with gifts—some small, and others were large. Their dinner table was bright and beautiful. Louise, his wife, is a good cook and she had baked a turkey with all the trimmings.

On Christmas Eve Lester suggested the two of us go shopping and pick up a few extra gifts. He wanted to be sure everyone had something nice under the tree. As we crossed the street from Robertson's department store over to the bank, I told him there was a young man in Alexandria, Louisiana, who wanted me to marry him. Lester stopped in the middle of the street and laughed out loud. "Bring him up here and let's look him over!"

When we returned to Lester's home, he took Mother to one side and said, "Who is this Jim Murphy? What's this about?" She said, "Oh, he's just a country boy with a heart of gold." He said, "Do you realize that he wants Sis to marry him?" Mother said, "Oh yes, I know all about it. She hasn't tried to keep anything secret. She reads all of his letters to me and tells me what he says to her on the phone." Lester said, "I want Sis to bring him up. I want to see what he is like." Since my brother was giving up his church, we were happy to be close to South Bend so we could be near him and his family the last months they were in the States.

We had an enjoyable Christmas with my brother and his family. The following morning we returned to Rochester, Indiana, which was fifty miles south, to prepare for the trip to Louisiana. We had one week to get ready and drive down south.

The New Year's Eve revival began with a building full of people. The Spirit of the Lord was very real as we prayed the old year out and the new year in. The church furnished us a comfortable place to stay. A few days after arriving in Shreveport, I telephoned Edith Mae Pennington, a lady preacher that pastored in the city. We had been close friends for many years. I had an appreciation for her sincere dedication to the Lord's work. She had been "Miss America" in the twenties and gave up all the glamor and popularity to be a gospel preacher. While we were talking she said, "The Lord showed me a young man is going to come into your life." I said, "I wish I was sure, but I am not." "I will pray for you," she said.

In a few days she called back. When I answered the phone she was laughing, "I am sure this is the man!" She went on to say, "While I was praying, the Lord gave me a vision. I saw the two of you standing in a field. A large shaft of light enveloped both of you and a wedding ring came down from heaven through the light and encircled the two of you and you became one!"

I was still uncertain. Jim phoned that he would be driving to Shreveport to attend the revival. He arrived late. I told Jim to follow us to the church. "When we get to church, don't let anyone know that you have come to see me or that you know me. I am very serious concerning God's work. I feel sure if it were known a young man was visiting who was romantically interested in me, it would hinder the revival." He said, "Alright, I'll be careful."

When he arrived at the church. he sat on the back seat. The pastor walked up to Jim and said, "Hi, where are you from?" He said, "I'm from Alexandria Air Base." The pastor said, "We're glad to have you in the meeting. We have a lady preacher and I am sure you will enjoy her ministry. Would you like to meet her?" He said, "Yes, I would." The pastor brought me back and introduced us. After we were introduced I returned to the platform. Neither of us showed any emotion. I had warned him before going to church to be careful and he was!

After church he followed us back to the apartment. He visited with Mother and me and then went to a nearby motel for the night. The following morning Jim came to the apartment and I began to prepare the noon meal for the three of us when the telephone rang. It was Sister Pruitt, a close friend I had known for many years. She called to tell me she had cooked a roast beef with all the trimmings. She and her husband wanted to bring the food to our apartment so we could share the meal together. She said, "I have vegetables and all kinds of good food so don't you prepare anything."

That was good news except Jim was there and no one was to know. I said, "That will be O.K." "Good," she said, "We will be there within an hour." I explained our plight to Jim.

There was a Dairy Queen on the corner. I told him, "You drive to the Dairy Queen and park until these people finish bringing the food in. Then you come back, ring the door bell and I will handle it from there." He was willing to cooperate. He went to the corner and waited. Finally he saw our friends bring the food in. So he came back to the house and rang the door bell. I answered and spoke real loud. "Oh! Brother Murphy, please come in." I introduced him to the Pruitts, telling them we met in the Alexandria revival. Fortunately, the Pruitts were not in the meeting the night before.

The two men had a wonderful time of fellowship together. Brother Pruitt invited Jim to their home anytime he was visiting in Shreveport. They gave him their address and phone number. The revival closed without anyone knowing Jim came to see me.

Houston and Leona

Jim & Leona cutting their wedding cake

My brother Ernest giving us marital advice at our reception. "It is the little digs that make a matrimonial grave."

5

THE CROSSROAD

We returned to Rochester to pastor the church. Letters and telephone calls from Jim were more frequent. When I received a letter from him, he always seemed to be so sure. Before putting an answer in the mail, I would get on my knees and pray, "Lord, if this is not the man for me and I am not the right one for him, let me say something in my letter that will make him know I am not the person he should marry. Please don't allow either of us to make the wrong decision."

Jim received his discharge papers from the Air Force in January, and returned to his home in Oklahoma. A few days later, I received a phone call from him saying he wanted to come to Indiana, and was praying I would be willing to become his wife. After all the broken marriages I had counselled, I felt that preaching the gospel and helping those with broken homes was as close to marriage as I wanted to get. I told Jim, "I will never marry you or anyone else unless the Lord shows me it is His will." He answered, "I am a Christian and God did show me that it is His will for us to get married. Please don't fight against God." He promptly blew me apart when he said, "God told me the two of us are to be together and the two of us were to work together in the ministry.

Two days later, I received a phone call and Jim was on the line. "I want to come to Indiana to talk with you."

"Yes, I want you to meet my brother, Lester."

"When I come up, will you promise to marry me?"

"Oh. . .no, no, no, there are a lot of things to be considered. You see, I can't promise to marry you until my brother talks with you. I want to be sure this is what God wants. Will you make me a promise? My brother is a godly man and if he feels it is God's will, we will get married; if he doesn't, will you go back to Oklahoma and forget that we ever met?"

Jim agreed to my terms. He said, "I know I am moving in the will of God and I am not afraid of any kind of test." He set the date he would come to Indiana. Due to a funeral, he didn't arrive on the day he had planned. My brother phoned and asked, "Has that guy from Oklahoma arrived?" I said, "No!" He began to tease me and said, "Maybe he's found another girl in Oklahoma that he has decided to marry." I said, "That would be alright. I am only interested in God's will concerning my getting married."

It was past 6 o'clock the following evening when I heard his car pull into the drive. That night my brother called and asked, "Have you heard from the guy from Oklahoma?" I said, "Would you like to talk to him?" He said, "Come on, stop kidding me." Jim came to the phone. Lester invited the three of us to come to South Bend the following day for the noon meal.

When we arrived, my brother was at the church. Little Frank and Stephen were babies at the time. They ran in and got on Jim's lap and began to talk and show him their toys. They were having a great time. All at once I heard Frank call out, "Uncle Jim, do you like this?" My sister-in-law laughed and said, "Yes, I told the boys they were getting a new uncle and his name was Jim; so they would have to call him Uncle Jim.

My brother walked in and I introduced Jim and Lester. I excused myself and walked back to the kitchen. I knew it would be a difficult time for Jim because he was under intense scrutiny. The two of them had visited less than thirty minutes when Lester said to Jim, "I have a toy for little Stephen and I want to put it together. I will run down in the basement and get some tools."

I was standing in the doorway that led to the basement when he walked past. He said, "Sis, I think this is our man." To say I was shocked is putting it mildly. While we were having lunch, Lester asked Jim a lot of questions and Jim gave a lot of answers. He made no attempt to impress my brother's family, neither did he strain for acceptance.

After the meal my brother asked Jim if he would like to walk across the street to see the church. The two men walked over to the church and there happened to be a man from the church who was waiting to see him. When they walked in, Lester shook hands with the man and said, "I want you to meet Jim Murphy. He's my future brother-in-law. He and my sister plan to be married." Jim told me later he almost fainted. He knew he was there under inspection and wondered what my brother thought about him. He thought to himself, "This is going to settle our getting married."

The man, who just happened to be the owner of a jewelry store, turned to Jim and said, "Oh great! Do you have your wedding rings?" Jim answered, "No." The man said, "I am going to bring out several diamonds. They will differ in size. You can make your choice. I will let you have them at cost. Do you want white or yellow gold?" By this time Jim was almost in shock and he could hardly speak. He looked at my brother and said,

The Crossroad

"I don't have any idea." "Get on the telephone and ask her!" said Lester.

Jim phoned the parsonage and asked for me. Then he told me the story about the jeweler. "Now, your brother said for you to make a choice. Will it be white or yellow gold?" I thought to myself, "This is a quick decision!" Was I ready for this commitment? I had to make up my mind. Am I going to marry this guy or not? I began to pray almost desperately for help and guidance. Then I said, "I think yellow gold would be nice." He said, "Alright." Shortly after, the owner of the jewelry store brought out several cards with different size diamonds from which I picked out what I thought was a nice diamond. In a few days the man returned with the ring.

We began to make plans for our marriage. Jim didn't want to go back home until after the wedding. He went to Kingsbury, Indiana and got a job. He rented an apartment a few blocks from the parsonage. After introducing him to the church, I told them we were planning to get married, and that he was living in an apartment. I made everything clear so that there would be no room for criticism.

One day my brother Lester came in and said, "I have to know the date you plan be married." I asked him when he was leaving for Philippines. He said, "It is impossible for me to be in Indiana after May 24th. This will be your last opportunity for me to perform the wedding or you will have to get someone else." "Ok, it will be the 24th."

He said, "I can see you are not sure. Sis, God knows our future. Mother is getting old. Soon the Lord will take her to heaven. I feel God has brought a Christian man into your life who will be good to you and will love you. Get your wedding gown and make the arrangements for the cake, flowers, and everything that is needed." I said, "I am not getting a wedding gown. I am going to be married in a tailored suit." Louise, Lester's wife, said, "Oh no! You must wear a gown! Try my wedding gown on. I am sure it is about your size." So, I tried the gown and it fit as though it had been made for me.

We rented the Methodist Church with a beautiful hall for the reception. The ladies from the South Bend church offered to be responsible for the decorations, music, etc.

6

OUR WEDDING DAY

The alarm clock began to ring.

I opened my eyes and my first thought was, "This is my wedding day!"

I reached for my robe and slippers.

I could hear voices in the kitchen.

Someone had made coffee.

The house soon became alive with activity.

It seemed that everyone was trying to talk at the same time. I took the bridal gown and veil out of the clothes closet and began to get dressed. Turning to me,

Mother said it was getting late, and then someone called from the living room, "It's time to go to the church!" They drove the car up to the side entrance. As the bridesmaids were meeting together, they commented on how beautiful everything was. Mrs. Louise White was playing the organ. The ushers had escorted the guests into the auditorium. At any moment the minister and ushers would be entering to see the bridal party walk down the aisle. Houston, my oldest brother, was giving me away. Ernest, my middle brother, was the best man. Lester, my youngest brother, was to perform the wedding.

It was soon after we had arrived that we learned everyone was there, EXCEPT JIM. My brother, Lester, began to be concerned when everyone began asking, "Where is Jim? What could have delayed him?" Lester suggested he drive over to Jim's apartment to see why Jim was delayed. When Lester arrived, he found that Jim was having a serious problem. He had rented a tuxedo and the company failed to put all the necessary items in to complete his outfit, such as the trousers, cummerbund, and cuff links.

Our Wedding Day

Lester departed quickly to retrieve the much needed items and returned with them in hand.

After helping Jim get ready, they hurriedly dashed off to the church and all that the guests knew was that the bride was fifteen minutes late coming down the aisle. Everyone said the wedding was just beautiful!

Our friends gave us many lovely gifts. As we were leaving the church, a large yellow box was handed to us. We were told to open it before leaving on our honeymoon. When we opened the box, to our happy surprise, it was packed with $5, $10, and $20 bills! There was more than enough cash to finance our entire honeymoon!

On our honeymoon we drove Louise, Lester's wife, and their two boys, Frank and Steve, to Denver, Colorado. It was late in the afternoon before we left Rochester to start our honeymoon. We drove a little over one hundred miles before stopping to get a motel.

The next day we arrived in Springfield,

Missouri, at Lester's home, so Louise could pack the things she was taking to the Philippines. Our route took us on through Oklahoma, Kansas, and into Colorado.

The trip through the Rocky Mountains was beyond my imagination! The blending of purple, blue, mauve, pink, and light greens of the mountains showed God's handiwork and was so thrilling I could hardly take it in! I was so excited that I cried, laughed, moved this way and that in my car seat, and could not imagine that each mountain seemed more beautiful than the previous one we passed!

We wanted to see Pike's Peak at Colorado Springs, but because of weather conditions, the lift was not in operation the day we were there, and we were advised not to drive up as conditions were not safe.

The following morning we left for Denver, where Lester was to meet us. When he arrived there, he had purchased a car which he planned on taking to the mission field. The next day he and his family drove to the coast and boarded a steamship to Manila, Philippines. Jim and I left the same day to return to Rochester, Indiana.

The honeymoon was behind us! As I envisioned my life as a homemaker, I found myself shopping for china patterns and brand-name furniture, but it did not take long for me to realize that a happy marriage does not consist of things.

In planning my life, I found direction before marriage by searching God's Word concerning my choice of a partner. God gives us the responsibility of picking our own mate. When you know what God's Word says, then act upon it correctly and your marriage will be a success!

7

THE UNEQUAL YOKE

Marriage is God's idea. However, God forbade marriage between believers and unbelievers because of the consequences. It is the most intimate relationship of human society.

Among the many hindrances to a thorough consecration, being unequally yoked is one of the greatest. "Be ye not unequally yoked together with unbelievers: for what fellowship hath righteousness with unrighteousness? and what communion hath light with darkness? And what concord hath Christ with Belial? or what part hath he that believeth with an infidel? (II Corinthians 6:14-15)

God said through Moses "Thou shalt not sow thy vineyard with divers seeds:

lest the fruit of thy seed which thou hast sown, and the fruit of thy vineyard, be defiled. Thou shalt not plow with an ox and an ass together. Thou shalt not wear a garment of divers sorts, as of woollen and linen together." (Deuteronomy 22:9-11)

The "unequal yoke" is holding back many from following Christ. God says, "Come out from among them...and be my sons and daughters." (II Corinthians 6:17-18) That is to say, "Get your neck out of the unequal yoke, and I will acknowledge you as one of My children." We know that we do not become children of God by any act of merit on our part. Separation from forbidden things can never save one's soul. On the other hand, here and in Matthew 5:44-45, we see man's responsibility as a child of God. If I yoke myself with darkness, unrighteousness, Belial, idols, or an infidel, I am morally and publicly identified with them, and not with God at all.

There are distinct phases in which "the unequal yoke" may be contemplated; domestically, commercially, and religiously. Some would confine the application to the first of these, but the apostle's words do not set any such limit.

BELIEVERS AND UNBELIEVERS CANNOT MIX

What pen can portray the mental anguish, the moral misery, and the spiritual tragedy flowing from a Christian's marriage with an unconverted person. I suppose nothing can be more deplorable than to wake up to the fact that you are linked for life with an unbeliever. The Christian longs to feed on God's Word, while the sinner craves the world. Eventually they will both starve. In unequally yoked marriages the unbeliever, in most cases, succeeds in converting the Christian to his way of living.

A Christian who has yoked himself in ignorance can be forgiven, but as a disciple he may never recover his loss. Most likely he will have a burdened life, a jeopardized character, and a hindered testimony.

Moreover, in domestic life it produces nothing but melancholy. Two persons who have joined together in the closest and most intimate relationship, with tastes, habits, feelings, desires, tendencies, and objectives are constantly grating one against the other. Unless the Christian further grieves the Lord by compromising, it produces estrangement, coldness, distance, and misunderstanding. The effect upon their children is equally sad. There can be no union of heart in the training of the children. One parent desires to bring them up for the Lord, the other for the world—and the children are almost sure to follow the unconverted parent.

How can this happen to a Christian? It happens when we forget the words of the Lord Jesus, "When thine eye is single, thy whole body is also full of light." (Luke 11:34) If our lives are governed by one objective—namely, to glorify and honor our Lord—we would never get into such perplexity. Whenever I am in doubt as to my path, I have reason to suspect that my eye is not single. If you have chosen a wrong path, do not ask God for guidance along that path, but turn off of it at once.

Many couples, though not "unequally yoked" are, at the least, very badly matched. Their tempers, tastes, habits and views are totally different, keeping the home in turmoil and dishonoring the Lord's name. This could have been avoided if the Christian's objective in life would have been to glorify God before personal interest or affection.

How easily the poor human heart persuades itself of the rightness of any step it desires to take, and how the devil furnishes arguments to help! One of my own sisters married a man who pretended to be a Christian in order to win her hand. What a sad awakening when she discovered, after marriage, that his profession was not sincere and that his heart was entirely of the world!

My friend, let nothing induce you to yoke yourself with an unbeliever. As soon as you have taken the step, your heart will be assailed by hopeless regrets. Rather, cry out to God for your affections to be altered by His power if they are wrongly placed, and sacrifice your temporal interests for them. It will be in your eternal interest to do so.

8

IN-LAWS

Your relationship to your partner's family is important. Occasionally the parents will be so ideal that you never have problems with them, but frankly, that is an exception rather than the rule. Most parents find it difficult to clip all apron strings after their children marry, even though they know they should.

It is hard for some to accept, but you do marry your partner's family. A couple should live separately from their parents, but be very respectful toward them. You have heard the expression, "No house is large enough for two women." It is natural for parents to offer advice based on their many years of experience, and sometimes couples rebel at this even to the point of rejecting good advice because it came from one of their parents.

Usually you get along with your own parents better than with your partner's parents, simply because you understand them better. Many times an in-law's suggestions appear to be disapproval or judgment when in reality they were given with the best of intentions.

You can afford to be considerate and thoughtful of your partner's parents. After all, they spent many years and thousands of dollars preparing your mate. The least you can do is treat them with dignity and respect. Avoid speaking negatively to your partner's parents; if it is necessary to tell them they are interfering too much in your marriage, *always let their own offspring state the situation.*

Mothers frequently have greater difficulty giving up their sons than do fathers their daughters. A loving wife should try to understand this and not put her husband into the difficult position of having to choose the one to whom he will be loyal, his wife or his mother. By being thoughtful and loving, the wife can help the husband maintain a relaxed feeling toward his parents, particularly his mother. This consideration will also benefit the wife. She can afford to be generous in this area. She has her husband much longer than his mother had him, and besides, she has a relationship to him that can never be shared by another woman, including his mother.

A husband should be very careful to avoid comparisons between his wife and his mother. It is entirely unfair to compare a young wife's ironing, cooking, and housekeeping abilities to those of a woman who has had twenty-five or thirty years of experience. Unkind comparisons of this nature will only create hostilities and conflict between the two women most important to the husband.

Difficulties in family relationships should be talked over carefully and dealt with lovingly. It is possible, with God's help, to have an enjoyable relationship with the in-laws that, in turn, enriches your marriage.

Many a joke has been made about wives who came to the table with rollers in their hair, sleepy eyes and unpowdered faces. Appearance isn't everything, but nevertheless, it is important. The Bible tells us that "man looketh on the outward appearance, but the Lord looketh on the heart" (I Samuel 16:7). Since your partner is human, he or she is going to look on your "outward appearance." It is therefore important that you do not use a wedding certificate as an excuse to relax your standards of appearance.

Before marriage, your partner would not have been attracted to you if you were not clean and neat in appearance. Help keep your partner's love alive by continuing to look well-groomed whenever possible. Your mate wants to be proud to introduce you to his or her friends, so don't make your partner feel like apologizing for your appearance.

Men have a natural tendency to relax on their day off by not shaving. A look in the mirror will reveal that he scarcely looks his best in his unshaven condition. It is usually selfishness that causes a man not to shave on the day that he is with his wife, because it is easier for him.

COURTESY

Courtesy and manners are a grace that should become a part of every Christian's life, but in our modern civilization they seem to be a dying art. A child is taught courtesy by his parents. It is something a girl can demand from her boyfriend, but the obvious time to discuss your differences in this matter is before marriage. Poor table manners and lack of normal courtesies can be a great source of irritation.

My mother insisted that the boys always wear a shirt to the table, that we refrain from putting our elbows on the table, say please to one another, and use good manners in our treatment of each other. She said, "You will never be in better company than the company you are in right now." I am most grateful for her insistence upon these things. All women enjoy being treated with courtesy and politeness.

A woman likes to be treated like a lady; therefore, a husband should be very careful to give his wife flowers and candy even after they are married. It is a wise husband who opens doors, including car doors, for his wife and treats her as a gentleman should treat a lady. You will be making an investment in her happiness and self-respect, which will increase her love for you. Since love begets love, this is one of the best investments you can make in your marriage.

LOYALTY

One almost inexcusable practice in marriage is disloyalty. Have you ever been out socially and heard a wife or husband berate and criticize his partner in front of mutual friends? This embarrassing practice is engaged in by partners who seek the safety of the group to vent their pent-up wrath. It is one of the most damaging things a person can do to his mate.

Be careful that you never, ever, air your partner's shortcomings, weaknesses, or deficiencies in front of other people. First, rehearsing grudges or nursing gripes stamp them more indelibly upon your mind. Second, the desire for approval is one of the basic drives of man.

If you are displeased with your partner's behavior in a matter, there are only two with whom you should share it: God and your partner. "But I have to have someone I can tell my problems to," is the usual answer. As a Christian, you have someone to whom you can take your problems—your heavenly Father. Then through prayer and the leading of the Holy Spirit, share the problems with your partner. If this does not work, consult your pastor or counselor.

9

BUILDING A CHRISTIAN HOME

"So ought men to love their wives
as their own bodies.
He that loveth his wife loveth himself."
—Ephesians 5:28

A happy home doesn't just happen. Each spouse has to make proper adjustments to his or her mate. God's plan is for a man and woman to be joined in marriage and that each one give of himself to make the other happy. Our daily differences and problems do not automatically solve themselves. I found that living with Jim becomes a daily demonstration of giving of myself for the good of both of us.

It did not take long for both of us to learn that each of us had our human imperfections and that no husband ever had a perfect wife, and no wife ever had a perfect husband. I prayed to the Lord to help me focus a lot of attention on the special man whom I had married. I believe that women have to be more flexible than men in a marriage relationship. I knew my life would not always be filled with excitement every day and every moment, and that as Christians our lives should be on an even keel as much as possible. I was aware that even the finest marriages experience some highs and some lows.

I realized before we married that Jim was so much in love with me that he only saw the good side of me. But what would he see after the excitement of the wedding wore off? When we began to see our mate's peculiarities, would we be gentle, kind, patient, and self-controlled while adjusting to each other?

Marriage can either be a happy or a very unhappy experience. This is when the Holy Spirit helps us turn weaknesses into positive attributes. Spirit-filled Christians have more enjoyment in their marriages when they allow the Holy Spirit to help them overcome their weaknesses. The Holy Spirit also gives grace to overlook, and to be happy in spite of any flaws our mate might have. Next to our relationship with God, the most wonderful relationship one can have is a happy home.

Weaknesses in one companion can further irritate a weakness in the other. If you desire to enrich your marriage, you must make an effort. The common complaint I hear from many couples is that they cannot communicate. I know that volumes have been written about the communication gap. Numerous individuals refuse or are afraid to discuss their true feelings to those who are near them. I feel no one should be discouraged from discussing his problems with his mate. Communication is more than a verbal expression. I ask questions and give Jim an opportunity to open up and express himself and tell about his problems. . .his likes, and dislikes. . .and by God's help we have been able to come up with the right solution. Above all, we learned to seek God's help through prayer and found that divine wisdom is available for the asking.

There is a huge difference between putting words together and conveying understanding. God has given me the ability to be sensitive to Jim's needs and feelings without him having to say anything. It is a gift from God to have the ability to feel another person's pain.

"So ought men to love their wives as their own bodies. He that loveth his wife loveth himself" speaks of a similar but much deeper sensitivity. It speaks of compassion.

Being sensitive to another person's feelings helps the communication process on every level. It is very unfortunate, but it is an ability that is neglected and discouraged in our modern world today.

Every person I have counseled with has one desire; he wants his home to be filled with peace and love, and not turmoil and bickering.

God designed the opposite sexes to complement each other and He planned marriage for man's good. The best advice on marriage is found in the Bible. "And the Lord God said, It is not good that the man should be alone; I will make him an help meet for him." Adam said, "This is now bone of my bones, and flesh of my flesh: she shall be called Woman, because she was taken out of Man. Therefore shall a man leave his father and his mother, and shall cleave unto his wife: and they shall be one flesh" (Gen. 2:18, 23-24).

God ordained the home as a place of emotional safety, but because of individual differences, gradually conflict comes into a relationship. If we don't learn how to resolve the conflicts, then our love will be replaced by hostility, hatred, and animosity, which will reduce our chances for a happy marriage and emotional security.

God's plan is that the home should be a place of love, security, and acceptance. "Where no counsel is, the people fall: but in the multitude of counsellors there is safety" (Proverbs 11:14). When you run into problems you are unable to solve, seek counsel from your pastor or a Christian counselor, but most of all, seek counsel from Christ. We can go straight to Christ of whom Isaiah wrote, "His name shall be called Wonderful, Counsellor..." (Isaiah 9:6).

Get counsel from the Word of God. You ought to study the Scriptures as to what is required in marriage. Psalm 119:24 says, "Thy testimonies also are my delight and my counsellors."

TRUST

Trust is commitment. In marriage we have to make a commitment to our marriage vows, a commitment to the Word of God as our counselor, and a commitment to the Lord Jesus.

"Trust in the Lord with all thine heart; and lean not unto thine own understanding. In all thy ways acknowledge him, and he shall direct thy paths" (Proverbs 3:5-6)—even in your marriage. Do that in your relationships with your wife, your husband, and your children. Trust is the secret of a happy marriage. All of life is bound up with the ethic of trust.

Trust is not only the secret of successful business, social and marriage relationships, it is equally important in our spiritual relationships. We are to trust in the Lord Jesus Christ for our salvation. He died on the cross and took our sins, and God raised him from the dead that we might have eternal life.

God ordained marriage, and intends our marriages to be successful. That doesn't always mean that all marriages will be happy. Our purpose in life is not to pursue happiness. Our purpose is to glorify God, to obey God even if we are not happy. Our lives are not always going to be filled with excitement every day and every moment. The Christian life is not that way. Read the Psalms. One day the Psalmist was elated, and another day he was depressed. Our Christian lives should be on an even keel as much as possible, but we will experience some dips and some highs. And that will also be true in the finest marriages.

LOVE

The Bible says that we are to "train up a child in the way he should go: and when he is old, he will not depart from it." (Proverbs 22:6) Every day that we live is a period of character development. We need to spend time with our children and love them and teach them the value of authority and discipline.

DISCIPLINE

We are not to discipline our children in anger. The Bible says, "Don't provoke your children to anger." (Colossians 3:21) Love them! But there needs to be discipline in the home. If there's no authority in the home, then the children will break even civil authority when they branch out in life.

AUTHORITY

Perhaps we have had so much teen-age delinquency and so much teen-age rebellion because our teenagers haven't had any authority in the home. We have abdicated our responsibility as parents. And one of the reasons for that is that we don't trust in the authority of God. We have God's authority to back us up in our authority as parents. Trust expects results that are the best for our families.

PATIENCE

Showing patience with our partners is a part of faith and trust. You can't judge an apple in June. You have to wait until September or October. The Bible teaches us that we are to have patience with our children and keep their love at all costs. If your heart is breaking, don't give up— have patience and perseverance.

As parents, husbands and wives, we grow through crisis periods if we don't allow the crises to destroy and separate us. Your marriage can become stronger through the difficulties that you may be having.

THE DIFFERENCE

Does Jesus Christ live in your home? Does he live in your heart? Many homes that have not split up are living in tension. The couples have not divorced, but they have no communication, and no real happiness in their homes. They have no unity, no joy. What a difference Christ can make! But the change will have to start with you: you as a wife, you as a husband, or you as a teenager, giving your heart and your life to Christ.

He wants to come into your heart and help you, save you, forgive you and give you the gift of eternal life. How wonderful!

Wouldn't it be great to have all the mistakes and failures of your life forgiven? Wouldn't it be wonderful to know that all your past sins have been wiped out by God so that he will never remember them against you?

Thousands of couples have found peace and joy and communication because of their relationship to Jesus Christ. And so can you, if you put your confidence and your faith in him. Husbands and wives, wouldn't you like to give your lives to Christ today? Wouldn't it be wonderful to hug your wife or your husband and say, "Darling, let's start all over. Let's make a new beginning!"

And you young people, who may have been causing some difficulty and heartache to your parents, your answer to a successful and joyful life is found in Jesus Christ!